I WANT TO BE A VETERINARIAN

Written by
Jonathan Reule

Illustration
Caballero Peza Mauricio
&
Caballero Peza Gabriel Fernando

Storyboard
Christiane Tee

First paperback edition May 2023
ISBN 978-981-18-6527-5

Published by Unibino Pte. Ltd.
31 Rochester Drive Level 3, #03-47 Singapore 138637

www.unibino.com

SERVICE DOG
Throughout history, animals have held a special place in our hearts. They're not just pets, but friends who often love us as much as we love them. To many, animal companions are cherished members of the family who provide comfort, joy, and camaraderie. Whether it's a loyal dog who greets you at the door or a cuddly cat who purrs in your lap, the bond between humans and animals is a truly special one.

This is why having trained Veterinarians who can help keep our pets alive and healthy is so meaningful in our modern society. A Veterinarian is usually the first person people will run to when their pets show signs of illness or disease. Unlike humans who can communicate with doctors, animals need a professional, like a veterinarian, who can identify these problems through their learning and experiences.

Have you ever wondered how we became such good friends with animals? It might surprise you to know that, at first, many animals were actually our enemies! House cats used to be fierce lions and tigers, stalking us through dense jungles and forests, while dogs were packs of wolves who were coordinating attacks, sometimes against us. But over time, something amazing happened.

We grew to respect and understand one another. Can you imagine the first person who bravely offered a piece of meat to a hungry wolf, who was once seen as a fierce predator? Or the first wild cat who slowly learned to trust humans after getting a spare fish or two when we returned from fishing trips? And let's not forget about the wise old owl who kept our food supplies safe by snatching up pesky mice! These little acts of kindness helped us realise that we could benefit from having animals around us.

And in time, animals learned to trust us too, allowing us to form a symbiotic relationship that benefited us both. This bond created a special fondness, and we began to watch out for one another. However, some cultures went beyond mere affection for animals to the point that they began to worship them as divine beings.

Take the Ancient Egyptians for example. They viewed cats as sacred creatures and incorporated them into their art, religion, and daily life. Archaeologists have discovered numerous tombs where cats were buried alongside their owners, suggesting that the Egyptians believed in an afterlife for animals as well as humans. In fact, the goddess Bastet was depicted as a woman with the head of a cat and was considered the goddess of fertility, love, and protection. The Egyptians believed that by honouring and caring for cats, they were earning the favour of the gods.

As our relationship with animals continued to grow more intertwined, we not only benefited from their protection and companionship but also from their ability to provide for our daily needs. We began to herd animals like sheep, cattle, and chickens to meet our daily needs. Sheep gave us wool to make clothes, cows provided us with milk to drink, and chickens laid eggs for us to eat.

However, caring for these animals also presented challenges. Like any living creature, they would fall ill, and we needed to find ways to nurse them back to health. This led to the emergence of our first veterinarians, who filled the need for animal care and medicine.

While the history of veterinary medicine is often attributed to ancient Greece and Rome, there are earlier records of animal healers in other parts of the world. For example, in ancient Sumer, a man named Urlugaledinna was renowned for his expertise in animal medicine and is considered by many to be the 'founder of veterinarians' for his use of herbal remedies on his patients.

Whereas in ancient India, there was already a well-established system in place for animal welfare. More specifically, practices and methods for healing and treating animals like cattle, goats, and sheep. It is said that Sushruta, a famous physician of the time, was able to create Ayurvedic Medicines not only for humans but animals as well.

Although if we move forward in time to the ancient Roman Empire, we can witness the progress that the veterinary profession had made. During this era, veterinarians were highly esteemed by many Romans, with some even considering it a high-priority profession. These skilled healers were often enlisted in the army and would accompany troops to battlefields to offer their services during the heat of the fight.

These vets were found on the frontlines, rescuing injured horses and bringing those capable of walking back to a safe area where they could treat the animal's wounds. These army vets were also used to diagnose infections and other illnesses that steeds might catch while at war, which made them a crucial asset during any battle.

As we progressed into the middle ages, though, many of the herbal remedies fell by the wayside, resulting in more alternative or folk practices. In some cases, priests and other holy individuals would be consulted to help cure animals of illnesses. This was largely due to the fact that many believed priests or other mage-like individuals had magical powers that could be used to help heal sick animals or at least occult knowledge that could be put into practice to keep animals healthy.

Unfortunately, these weren't the best treatment for the ill animals involved. Yet, these were the only remedies that most commoners could afford. For many, animals were essential for daily life. Peasants needed horses, oxen, and mules to help plough their fields and transport goods to and from their farms.
Others needed pigs, sheep, and lambs for food sources and couldn't risk a deadly outbreak in their herds. As a result, consulting these alternative vets was often the only viable option for commoners seeking animal care.

Sadly, the elite often used the best-practising vets, leaving the folk and esoteric healers to commoners. Upper-class individuals could hire stable keepers and trained equine managers with years of experience and firsthand knowledge of animal wellbeing.

Most practices at this time were more preventive in measure rather than trying to cure animals after an injury or illness. Much of this involved tailoring the animal's diet to give it the best fitness it needed, along with giving animals proper living environments and sanitary conditions. But many practices were based on the stable manager's first-hand knowledge instead of being standardised across the field.

At least, that was the case until 1762, when Claude Bourgelat founded the first veterinary school of medicine in Lyon, France. For years, Claude had been working as the head of Lyon's Academy of Horsemanship, where he instructed students on how to best care for these animals, to keep them healthy and thriving. But during his time at the academy, he came up with an idea to start a school that would focus on the health and well-being of all animals, not just horses.

His idea soon became very popular due to an outbreak of a cow-related disease called Rinderpest, which began sweeping through the nation. The king of France at the time was then willing to give Claude a short-term loan for his school in the hopes that it might slow down the spread of the disease among cattle. Thanks to Claude and his school, he was able to temper the plague's full impact by showing how science and medicine could be used as more reliable treatments for animals.

In modern times, the field of veterinary medicine has grown tremendously, with veterinary schools now spread across the globe. These institutions play a critical role in training and educating the next generation of veterinarians, equipping them with the knowledge and skills needed to provide the best care for animals. As a result, animals are now receiving more advanced and specialised care than ever before.

On top of that, you'll find that both the medications and technologies used have changed and become more practical for our animal companions. There are whole research centres working to make medications for pets and animals, along with new technologies that allow Veterinarians to diagnose hard-to-see problems, like broken limbs or tumours in animals. All of these advances have made it easier for veterinarians to help many animal patients that may walk through their office doors.

With all this information, you might wonder what it takes to become a veterinarian. Firstly, it's important that you have the right type of temperament and are willing to work with pets and animals, even if they don't want to be around a vet whom they consider to be a stranger. You'll also need to understand that not all animals can be cured. Some will sadly be at the end of their lives when you consult with them and their owners.

Beyond that, you'll need to study hard and make sure you get the right college degree before applying to veterinary schools. The most popular majors for pre-vet students are the following: Animal Sciences, Biology, Chemistry, and Zoology. But once you're in, it's time to hunker down and study hard while at veterinary school.

Then after you've graduated, it's up to you to decide what type of veterinarian you'd like to be. If you didn't know, there are several branches within the veterinary field that require their own unique specialisations and expertise. Why don't we look at some of these options to see what interests you most?

Animal companion veterinarians are known for working with smaller animals, such as household pets like dogs, cats, birds, rabbits, and guinea pigs. So, if you've ever taken your pet lizard or rabbit to the vet, it's likely that this is the type of Vet you've visited. But these professionals need to be good problem solvers to find out what's wrong with the animals brought into their clinics because sometimes the answers aren't as straightforward as you might think.

Veterinary behaviourists are trained to understand animals deeply and why they behave the way they do. You'll often find these Vets working with pets and their owners to help change undesirable behaviours. This type of professional might work with aggressive animals who can't get along with others or help pets with high anxiety to relax when a storm is brewing outside.
They may even be called upon when animals stop eating their meals. This is why they need to deeply understand animal behaviour to know best what is going on in their minds.

Research veterinarians are often busy studying animals from a biological and chemical standpoint. These experts discover how different animals' immune systems work and how certain infections and diseases affect these creatures. These Veterinarians are often found in laboratories or working to make new medications. So when choosing this career, make sure you have a strong background in biology and chemistry!

Emergency veterinarians have to be ready for whatever type of animal may step into their office. These Vets work with emergency patients, often animals that are hurt badly or have eaten something poisonous! But these vets must think on their feet and act as quickly as possible when caring for their patients.

Specialists veterinarians focus on one specific aspect of care for their animal patients. Usually, these individuals further their training after veterinarian school to narrow in on one area of expertise that they will work in. You can find these vets working as animal surgeons, dermatologists, or even oncologists, but one thing they have in common is their specialised focus on their niche.

Being a veterinarian can be a demanding yet incredibly rewarding career. Whether you decide to specialise in animal behaviour, surgery, or research, there will always be a multitude of opportunities for growth and learning. The field of veterinary medicine is constantly evolving, and as such, there will always be new techniques and technologies to learn and implement.

However, it's important to note that being a veterinarian can also be a challenging career. Working with animals can be unpredictable and requires a great deal of patience, empathy, and problem-solving skills. So if you're considering a career in veterinary science, know that with dedication, hard work, and a love for animals, you can make a real difference in this world to many humans and animals alike!

Shubhi Saxena
Founder, Unibino

My Inspiration

As a parent in this ever-changing world, it can sometimes feel overwhelming when it comes to our children's futures. New technologies seem to be arising almost every day, and with so many innovations, it creates unique professions which many of us wouldn't have dreamed to be necessary only a few years ago. Which to me is a good thing. Because with so much variety, my children can have the opportunity to pick a career that will fit their personalities and build upon their strengths. As you may imagine, this desire within me to provide my children with the resources they needed to thrive, led me to search out books that would be easy enough for them to understand while teaching them about various professions.

Only, I found that these books were few and far between. Even if I could find a book about a certain profession geared towards young readers, I found them sparse inside and limited to only certain careers that may not fit my children's abilities. This is when I came up with the idea to write my own children's books, teaching them about all the various careers in the modern world. After months of researching different professions and learning more than I ever expected, I quickly realised this was going to be a bigger project than I first anticipated. I dove into the histories of these professions, discovering links to the past, and why these professions were now so important.

Ultimately my goal was to offer my children options, to show them that there is no one set path for everyone. But in this, I stumbled upon something bigger. I wanted to share this with future generations. To share with all children and parents about these careers, to help spark curiosity, and to instil a passion for the future. Everyone has special talents and abilities, and I hope that this series will be able to offer clarity and inspiration to children around the world. Because at the end of the day, it's never too early to start dreaming and never too late to take action. With this, I hope you enjoy this series and that your young ones become the best versions of themselves as they can achieve.

www.ingramcontent.com/pod-product-compliance
Ingram Content Group UK Ltd.
Pitfield, Milton Keynes, MK11 3LW, UK
UKHW060102300726
14090UKWH00003B/346

* 9 7 8 9 8 1 1 8 6 5 2 7 5 *